FLORA
IN HER KITCHEN

Flora Chiarello Menges

Illustrations by Kate Scheulen

Workwomans Press
Seattle

ISBN: 978-0-9820073-4-1

Cover photograph Flora Chiarello High School Graduation June 15, 1930
Back cover photograph: Flora's 3000 Christmas Cookies 1965

Third Printing June 2010

WORKWOMANS PRESS
Seattle
www.workwomanspress.com

FLORA IN HER KITCHEN

Lucia Longo Chiarello age 24 (1911)
Born December 11, 1887 Corsano, Italy
Died 1949

Two beans you are
Two beans you be
I see you are
Too beans for me.

—Flora Chiarello Menges
Christmas Bean Ceremony1986

PREFACE

It has been my pleasure to assist my aunt Flora in creating this cook-book. Together we have sorted through a lifetime of recipes, magazine clippings, 3x5 cards, and cookbooks marked by coffee stains and crumbs, to find Flora's favorites. We have cooked many of the recipes together, and Flora has demonstrated the art of making braided potato rolls and the cross-over tarallini cookies. At 96, her fingers are still nimble, and she is much more skillful and faster than I am at these culinary arts.

Flora's first cookbook was *The Silver Jubilee Supermarket Cookbook,* published in 1952 and dedicated to "Mamie Dowd Eisenhower." No surprise that the recipes here bring back the fifties. They represent home-cooking as my mother's generation practiced it. The recipes may be high in fat; they are certainly not meat- nor sugar-free. But experienced cooks will know how to make the appropriate substitutions, if they wish.

The bulk of the recipes represent Italian or Italian-American cooking. Others reflect the German-American tradition, equally important in the fifties, and one which Flora mastered in cooking for Ted Menges, her husband of German immigrant background. Several recipes have come from other family members and friends. My own father was a huge fan of Flora's cooking and he often sent me recipes which he had received from her.

Over the years, I have found that these recipes from Flora form the basis of my own repertoire. As I have cooked through this cookbook, I have learned new combinations and new tricks, even though, after fifty years, I might have thought I knew it all!

For those who want simple and familiar home cooking at its best, I offer to you these recipes of my beloved aunt Flora.

—Gail Chiarello, Spring 2010

FLORA'S MIRROR

Introduction by Susan Sherrell

Flora Chiarello grew up in a large Italian family in Albany, New York. Her oldest brother, my father, was born Libertario Chiarello in San'Arica, on Italy's Salentine peninsula. His parents, Biagio Chiarello and Lucia Longo, were from Corsano, at the tip of the peninsula. Biagio Chiarello's father had been the only man in Corsano who could read and write; he was called "il Notaro." My grandfather trained at a technical school to become a machinist and worked in France, Tunisia and Egypt before seeking his fortune in America. Libertario and his brother, Refrattario, emigrated to the United States with their mother in 1911 (Biagio had gone ahead two years earlier). In addition to Libertario, and Refrattario, they raised three more children, Flora, Artes (who subsequently renamed himself "Art"), Alba, and Sesto. Biagio was known by his father's old nickname—"il Notaro." Politically he was an anarchist; religiously, an atheist. He had no time for frivolities.

In 1939 Libertario married Elsie Trickey, of Rochester. Her father, Carlton Trickey, traced his lineage back to Tom Trickey, an Englishman who landed in New Hampshire in 1687, as we now suspect, fleeing the gallows of Newgate Prison. In upstate New York at that time WASPs ruled. Italian names were considered "funny." My mother convinced Dad to change his name to "Leo P. Sherrell." The middle initial, "P," stood alone; my father followed Harry S. Truman and his own father who had added "A" to "Biagio Chiarello," liking the abbreviation "ABC."

I grew up in Webster, New York, in an old community directly on Lake Ontario, Forest Lawn, separated from Lake Road by two stone pillars and a big grass playing field. We were a six hour drive from Albany. Dad would drive the old state highway 5-and-20, parallel to the Erie and Barge Canals, past Utica and Herkimer and Fonda, along the Mohawk River to Albany. There I found this "other family," who lived in a second floor flat with lace curtains, polished wood floors, and unfamiliar smells of garlic and tomato sauce. There was a globe in the living room, the Encyclopedia Britannica, a hand-carved chess set. Up a narrow stairway to the attic were naked ladies, representations of Aphrodite which my grandfather carved out of plaster or wood. The food tasted rich and different. The relatives were darker, deeper, warmer, more interesting than the people I was growing up with in Forest Lawn.

This Italian family loved my mother. When she died when I was two, my aunt Flora and my uncle Sesto drove me and my two sisters to my aunt Albi's, in Highland Park, north of Chicago, for the summer of 1950. We lived with Albi, her husband, Donald Diaz, and their daughter, Dawne, while Dad courted Eleanor DeVoe, who would become his new wife. Once remarried, he seemed to lose contact with his Italian family.

In June 1955 my aunt Flora and her husband, Ted (she was now Flora Menges), made a surprise visit to Forest Lawn to bake lasagna and a ricotta tart for my father's birthday. I was eight. This struck me as wonderful and unusual, a reminder of that other family I barely knew! My aunt Flora epitomized that other world. She had dark curly hair and glasses, like my sister Gail. She was a bookworm, but at the same time so much more glamorous than any of the women her age in Forest Lawn. She and Ted had traveled to faraway places like California. She had seen Bing Crosby enter a convenience store to buy cigarettes. A world in which movie stars did ordinary things in full view of other people—this reeked of sophistication. Being Italian also seemed a fantasy in those conforming nineteen fifties.

Flora's life had not been easy. Her father was smart, but he was a patriarchal tyrant who abused his wife and children. Life with him was unbearable. Flora hated the degrading way he spoke to them. At nineteen, she left home to live with her aunt, Eunice Longo, then rented her own room, working two jobs to pay for it. When her sister married Donald Diaz, she went to live with them. At thirty-one, Flora married Ted Menges, a bon vivant fifteen years her senior. Marriage to this self-centered older man was a challenge, but by then Flora had a good job as an accountant in New York State's tax division, and a wide circle of friends and family. A benefit—thanks to Ted Menges' German roots—was that Flora's cooking repertoire expanded to include many German-American favorites—sauerbraten, kugelhupf, apfelkuchen, mailanderlai, all of which will be found in this cookbook along with her Italian recipes.

After that birthday visit in 1955, I didn't see Flora again for decades. The Italian relatives disappeared from my life. It was not until my stepmother died in 1981 and my father made his first trip west, by train, to see his sisters, now living in southern California, and his West Coast daughters, that I reconnected with my aunts Flora and Albi. To my happy surprise, a warmth and rapport sprang up among us almost immediately. Flora and Albi became the women in my life who most helped mitigate the loss I had felt all those decades following my mother's death. They were smart, funny, good with money, and they dressed well. They represented a type of older woman I was not familiar with—competent, independent older women who were enjoying their lives. And they cooked fantastically.

My aunt Flora is the essence of warmth, caring, fun, humor, and--as you will see from this book--good cooking. Food with flavor, depth, richness—food coming from both the Italian and the German traditions, and cooked with love.

I'll close with a story. As my father aged, his visits to Flora were one of the few things that brightened his spirits, and when he could no longer take the train from Rochester to Albany alone, one of his daughters would drive him to visit his sister. I remember a trip in which I was the driver. We were sitting in Flora's living room. Dad was looking at himself in a hand mirror and commenting on how terrible he looked—deep circles under his eyes, ravages of age in his face. I remember Flora saying to him, "You are looking in the wrong mirror. Come and look at yourself in this other mirror. My mirror. It reflects you the way you really are, the way I see you. With the eyes of love."

Thank you, Flora, for your mirror, and for seeing with the eyes of love.

—*Susan Sherrell, Mother's Day, May 9, 2010*

TABLE OF CONTENTS

BREAKFAST & BREADS *13*

STARTERS & SALADS *25*

SOUPS *31*

VEGETABLES & VEGETARIAN DISHES *41*

MAIN COURSES *61*

COOKIES *77*

CAKES, PIES & OTHER SWEETS *89*

USEFUL TIPS *104*

INDEX *106*

Photographs

Lucia Longo Chiarello in 1911 *frontispiece*
A. Biagio Chiarello in 1920 *24*
La Famiglia Chiarello in 1923 *34*
Libertario Chiarello in 1914 *42*
Alba Chiarello Diaz in 1930 *62*
Seeing Pa Off in 1949 *78*
Flora Chiarello Menges in 1972 *88*

Chapter I

BREAKFAST AND BREADS

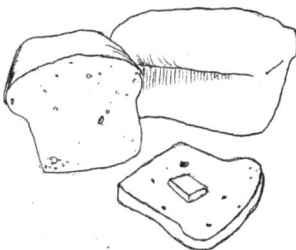

CORNED BEEF HASH

2 cups chopped cooked corned beef
2 cups chopped boiled potatoes
1 T minced onion
1/2 cup cream, milk, or stock
2 T butter

Mix together the corned beef, potatoes, onion, and liquid. Melt butter in a heavy skillet, add hash, and pat down evenly. Cook very slowly until browned on the bottom. Fold like an omelet and turn out onto a hot platter. If crisp brown bits are desired throughout the hash, scrap up the bottom occasionally. Serves 4.

POTATO PANCAKES

6 potatoes, grated
1 T flour
1/4 t baking powder
1-2 eggs, well-beaten
1 grated onion
1 t salt and a dash of pepper
1/3 cup oil or fat or bacon drippings
1 T butter

Sprinkle flour and baking powder over the grated potatoes. Add the egg, grated onion, salt and pepper, and mix until blended. Heat oil and butter in a heavy skillet and drop potato mixture by spoonfuls into the hot oil. Spread cakes so they are quite thin and cook 2-3 minutes on each side or until well done. Makes 10-14 pancakes.

COTTAGE CHEESE PANCAKES

3/4 cup sour cream
2 eggs
1/3 cup cottage cheese

1/2 cup sifted flour
1/2 t baking soda
1/2 t salt

Place all ingredients in a blender and process on low until smooth. Let stand 10 minutes. Bake on a buttered moderately hot griddle until brown. Yields: 8-10 small pancakes.

CRANBERRY MUFFINS

2 cups flour, or:
   1 cup white flour
   1/4 cup buckwheat flour
   1/4 cup whole wheat flour
   1/4 cup potato flour
1 cup sugar
1/4 cup buttermilk powder
   (optional, but good)
1/2 t baking soda
1 t ground nutmeg
1 t ground cinnamon
1/2 t ground ginger

1/2 t salt
2 t grated orange peel
1/2 cup butter
3/4 cup orange juice. or:
   1/4 cup orange juice
   1/4 cup apple juice
   1/4 cup yoghurt
2 eggs, beaten
1 T vanilla extract
1-1/2 cups coarsely chopped
   cranberries
1-1/2 cups chopped pecans*

In a large bowl, combine flour and sugar, buttermilk powder baking powder, baking soda, nutmeg, cinnamon, ginger, salt and orange peel. Cut in the butter until crumbly . Stir in the orange juice, eggs, and vanilla until just moistened; add cranberries and pecans.

Fill 18 greased or paper-lined muffin cups 2/3 full. Bake at 375º F for 20 minutes, or until golden. Makes 24 muffins.

*NOTE: Toast pecans in a small black iron skillet over medium heat, ahead of time. This brings out the flavor.

KUGELHUPF

Dough:
2 pkg dry yeast or cupakes
1/2 cup water
3/4 cup scalded milk
1 cup butter
1 cup sugar
1/2 t salt

4 eggs slightly beaten
4 cup flour
Grated rind of one lemon
1/4 cup blanched almonds
1/2 cup ea of diced citron, white
    raisins, and currants

Sprinkle dry yeast or crumble yeast cake into 1/4 cup water—using very warm water (105°-115° F) for dry yeast, lukewarm water (80°-90° F) for fresh yeast. Let stand a few minutes, then stir until dissolved. Add 1-1/2 cups flour; beat until smooth. Cover with a damp clean towel and let rise in a warm place for 1 hour.

With an electric beater, cream butter and sugar; add salt and grated lemon rind. Add eggs one at a time, beating well after each addition. Add yeast and remaining flour. Beat for 10 minutes. Butter a 9-in Turk's head pan (a fluted pan with a tube) and decorate bottom and sides with blanched almond halves. pour in half the dough; spinkle over the citrons, raisins, and currants; cover with the remaining dough. This should fill half the pan. Cover and let rise in a warm place until dough just reaches the top of pan. (Cake will be coarse and dry if allowed to rise too long.) Bake in a preheated 350° F oven 45-55 minutes. Cool in pan for 5 minutes; then carefully remove to cake rack. Serve sprinkled with powdered sugar.

APFELKUCHEN

Dough:
1 pkg dry yeast or cake
1/4 cup water
3/4 cup scalded milk
1/4 cup butter
1/4 cup sugar
1 t salt
2 eggs slightly beaten
2-3/4 cup flour

Topping:
5 peeled cooking apples
2 T melted butter
1/4 cup sugar
1/2 t ground cinnamon
2 T raisins
1/2 cup toasted chopped walnuts

Sprinkle dry yeast or crumble yeast cake into 1/4 cup water—using very warm water (105°-115° F) for dry yeast, lukewarm water (80°-90° F) for fresh yeast. Let stand a few minutes, then stir until dissolved. Stir scalded milk, 1/4 cup butter, sugar and salt altogether; let cool to lukewarm. Then add yeast mixture and eggs. Beat in 1-1/2 cups flour; cover with a damp clean towel and let rise in a warm place until doubled in bulk—about 40 minutes. Then stir in the remaining flour to make a very soft dough. Knead it gently on a floured board, adding more flour as needed to keep it just shy of sticky. Cover and chill for half an hour; then roll out the door and fit into a greased 9x12 baking pan.

Quarter and core the apples; cut into eighths or thinner. Press closely into the dough, making neat rows or, a daisy shape. Combined sugar, cinnamon and raisons and sprinkle over apples; then top with the toasted walnuts. Cover and let rise in a warm place until the dough springs back when touched lightly with finger. Bake in a preheated 350° F oven for 30-40 minutes.

POPOVERS

1 cup flour
2 eggs, unbeaten
1/4 t salt
1 t melted butter
1 cup milk

Put flour in a bowl, make a well in the center and drop in the salt.
Add milk gradually and stir well. When smooth, add the
unbeaten eggs and melted butter and beat until smooth.

Preheat muffins pans to hissing hot, or have ready hot
earthenware or glass cups, filling the pans 1/3 full. Bake in a hot
oven (450° F) for 30 minutes, then in a more moderate 350° for 15
more minutes.

Serve at once. Popovers when properly baked are mostly crisp
outer shell and only a very little moist material inside. Popovers
may be split and filled with creamed chipped beef or creamed
chicken for a special breakfast or supper dish. Makes eight.

CINNAMON TWISTS

1 pkg dry or 1 cube fresh yeast   Filling:
3/4 cup warm water (110–115° F) 1/4 cup melted butter
4 to 4-1/2 cups flour   1/2 cup brown sugar
1/4 cup sugar   4 t fresh ground cinnamon
1-1/2 t salt
1/2 cup warm milk (110° F)
1/4 cup soft butter
1 egg

Dissolve yeast in 1/4 cup warm water. Add remaining water, 2 cups flour, sugar, salt, milk, butter, and egg, and beat with an electric mixer or in a Cuisinart. Stir in enough remaining flour to form a soft dough. Turn onto a floured board and knead until smooth and elastic, about 6-8 minutes. Place in a greased bowl, turning once to grease the top. Cover with a clean damp towel and let rise in a warm place until double in bulk, about 1 hour. Punch down, and roll into a 16-in x12-in rectangle. Brush with butter. Combine brown sugar and cinnamon; sprinkle over butter. Let dough rest for 6 minutes. Cut lengthwise into three 16-in x 4-in strips. Cut each strip into sixteen 4-in x 1-in pieces. Twist and place on greased baking sheets. Cover and let rise until double in bulk, about 30 minutes. Bake at 350° F for 15 minutes or until golden.

FLORA'S POTATO ROLLS

1-1/2 sticks butter
2 cups mashed potatoes*
1/3 cup sugar
2 t salt
1 cup scalded milk

2 pkgs dry yeast
1/3 cup water heated to 105°-115°
6 cups all-purpose flour
4 eggs plus 1 egg yolk, beaten
1 egg white beaten with 1 t water

In a large bowl, add butter, sugar, salt and milk to hot potatoes. Cool to lukewarm. Dissolve yeast in warm water; add yeast water to lukewarm potato mixture. Gradually stir in 3 cups of flour. Add beaten eggs; mix until smooth. Add remaining flour 1/2 cup at a time, until dough is firm. Knead until a smooth ball is formed, adding flour as necessary to keep dough from sticking. Place dough in a large greased bowl, turning it to grease top of dough. Cover with a clean damp cloth. Let rise. Punch down 2-3 times and then flatten it.

"I weigh the dough. To make braided rolls, take 1 oz of dough and roll into a long rope. Cut the rope into a 1/3 piece and a 2/3 piece. Place the end of the smaller piece at the midpoint of the longer piece, and start braiding the 3 ends."—FCM.

Place on a baking sheet 1 in apart. Brush each roll with beaten egg. white and water mixture. Let rise in a warm spot until doubled in bulk. Bake at 425° F for 12-15 minutes.

NOTE: Mash potatoes by hand. Using a Cuisinart will turn potatoes to glue. Also, if adding butter or milk to mashed potatoes, subtract from butter and milk in recipe.

FLORA'S BREAD STICKS

Dough:
1 pkg dry yeast (1 cake fresh)
3/4 cup milk
1 T sugar
2 t salt
1 T soft butter or oil
1/4 cup warm water (110° F)

3 to 3-1/2 cups flour

Topping:
1 egg white, beaten
1 T water
Poppy or sesame seeds or
   coarse salt

Dissolve yeast in warm water. Scald milk; add sugar, salt and butter. Cool to lukewarm, then add to yeast with 1-1/2 cups flour. Beat with an electric mixer at medium speed until smooth, scraping the bowl. Add the remainder of the flour, first by spoon and then by hand, until dough leaves the sides of the bowl. Turn dough onto lightly floured board; knead until smooth. Place in lightly greased bowl; turn dough over to grease top. Cover with a damp clean cloth and let rise in a warm place until double in bulk, about 45 minutes.

Turn dough onto board and roll to a 16-in x 6-in rectangle. From the wide side, cut the dough into 1/2-in strips. Roll each strip by hand to make a pencil shape. Dough strips will be 8-in long. Place slightly apart on 2 greased baking sheets. Let rise in a warm place for 15 minutes. Mix beaten egg white with water and brush sticks with topping, sprinkling with seeds or coarse salt as desired. Bake in a hot oven (400° F) 10 to 15 minutes or until golden brown. Cool on wire racks. Makes 32 bread sticks.

A. Biagio ("Notaro") Chiarello age 40 (1920)
Born December 2, 1880 Corsano, Italy
Died 1973

Chapter II

STARTERS & SALADS

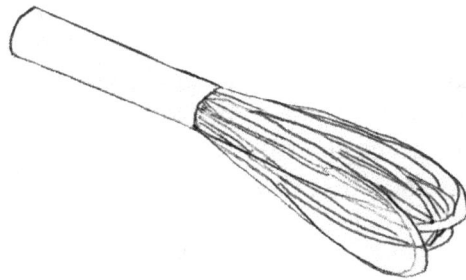

FLORA'S ANTIPASTI

Pile of lettuce
Can of pimentos or slices of fresh red pepper
Can of anchovies
Peperoncini (hot pepper)
Fresh white mushrooms cut in quarters
Salami
Provolone cheese
Mild yellow Greek peppers
Pickled beets
Slivers of celery or finocchio
Artichoke hearts
Pickled green beans
Fresh tomatoes (quartered)
Black and green olives
Cucumbers (thick slices or sticks)
Thin slices of white or purple onion
Capers
Caponata (see page 26)

Arrange the vegetables artistically on a platter on the pile of
lettuce. Criss-cross the anchovies over the mixture of vegetables.
Around the edges place the tomato quarters and the olives. A few
long green onions may be criss-crossed on top of the platter.

—FCM, May 24, 1986

MEINPAPA'S CUCUMBER SALAD

2-3 fresh sliced cucumbers, peeled, and cut into rounds.
Equal amounts of red wine vinegar & water or (Dad's preference)
    1/3 vinegar to 2/3 water
Salt
Italian herbs (oregano, basil, fresh from the garden)
Sliced onions (Walla Walla)
Chopped garlic cloves

Layer cucumbers, onions, garlic, herbs. Pour over red wine vinegar & water.   Repeat until all ingredients are used up.

Let sit a couple of days. Very refreshing!

MEINPAPA'S SALAD DRESSING

The main ingredients are oil and vinegar. The vinegar can be cider, red wine, or balsamic, whatever is on hand.

The proportions are 1/4 vinegar, 1/4 water, 1/2 olive oil. If the proportions vary, it's no big deal.

> *—Meinpapa, August 31, 2003*

FLORA'S PICKLED BEETS

4-5 medium beets
2 cups white vinegar
2 cups water
1/3 cup white sugar

1 onion, sliced
2 large garlic cloves (peeled)
1/4 t peppercorns
1 bay leaf, crumbled

Sterilize two quart canning jars, lids, and rings. Invert the jars on a clean towel, and set aside, with the lids and rings.

Place the vinegar, water, sugar, and canning salt in a saucepan and bring to boil, then set aside. Steam beets until a fork pierces them easily. Let cool, then rub off outer skins. Place one clove of garlic and a bayleaf at the bottom of each jar, with a few peppercorns. Slice beets, and add them with the sliced onions to the quart jars. Pour the vinegar-water mixture over the beets. Let stand a day or two in the refrigerator before serving.

NOTE: Will keep in the refrigerator for 2-3 weeks or longer.

GERMAN HOT POTATO SALAD (Kartoffelsalat)

6 medium waxy potatoes
4 strips minced bacon or 2 T
    bacon drippings
1/4 cup chopped onion
1/4 cup chopped celery
1 chopped dill pickle

1/4 cup water or stock
1/2 cup vinegar
1/2 t sugar
1/2 t salt
1/8 t paprika
1/4 t dry mustard

Cook potatoes in their jackets in a covered saucepan until tender.
Peel and slice them while they are still warm.

Heat the minced bacon or bacon drippings in a heavy skillet, and
add the onion and celery and sauté until brown.

Separately bring to a boil the water, vinegar, sugar, salt, paprika
and dry mustard. Then pour these ingredients into the skillet.
Combine with the potatoes and the dill pickles. Serve at once with
chopped parsley or chives.

COLE SLAW

2-pound head of cabbage
2 carrots, peeled
1/2 cup pineapple juice
1 cup mayonnaise
1 T sugar

2 T white vinegar
dash of salt
dash of white pepper

Remove outer leaves and core of the cabbage and shred the remainder. Dice the carrots very fine and add to the minced cabbage. Mix the mayonnaise, sugar, vinegar, salt and white pepper and combine with the cabbage and carrots. Serves 10.

FLORA'S CAPONATA

2 large eggplants, cubed
2 small zucchini, cubed
4 medium onions, chopped
3 large cloves garlic, minced
6 celery stalks, chopped
1 large can plum tomatoes

20 large green olives, pitted &
  quartered
1/2 cup vinegar
4 t sugar (or less)
1/2 cup capers
Olive oil

Fry the cubed eggplants and zucchini in olive oil under tender and set aside. Add chopped onions, celery and garlic to the pan and sauté until tender. Add plum tomatoes, olives, and capers. Mix sugar with vinegar and stir into vegetables. Cook until mushy. Can be served cold as a dip or as a condiment on the antipasto tray (see page 26).

ENDIVE & RADICCHIO SALAD

1 large head endive
1 small head radicchio, halved and sliced crosswise into 1/4-in.
   strips
2 T red wine vinegar
1 T Dijon mustard
Coarse salt
Freshly ground pepper
1/4 cup extra-virgin olive oil

Tear the endive into bite-size pieces and place in large bowl with
the radicchio and set aside. Whisk together the vinegar and mustard in a small bowl with the salt and pepper. Add the olive oil.
Just before serving, drizzle the vinaigrette over the salad and toss.

NOTE: Endive is also called "frisée," French for "curly" or
"frizzy."

La Famiglia 1923: Front row—Art, Alba, Sesto; Back row—Refrattario, Libertario, Flora; Seated—Lucia.

Chapter III

SOUPS

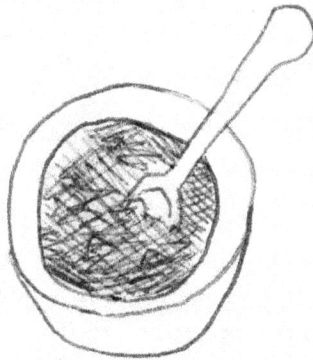

FRENCH ONION SOUP

1/4 cup butter
6 medium onions, sliced
1 quart boiling water*

5 bouillon cubes*
6 slices toasted French bread
1/2 cup grated Parmesan cheese

Melt the butter in a large saucepan, add the onions, and cook 10 minutes. Dissolve the bouillon cubes in the boiling water, and add this mixture to the onions. Cook over low heat until the onions are tender. Pour soup in an earthenware soup dish, place the toasted French bread on top; and sprinkle with the Parmesan. Bake in a hot oven (425° F) until the cheese melts. Yield: 6 servings.

*NOTE: Replace water and bouillon cubes with 1 quart brown stock.

PARADISE SOUP ("Zuppa di Paradiso")

3 stiffly beaten egg whites
3 slightly beaten egg yolks
3 t fine dry bread crumbs
3 T Parmesan cheese

2 sprinkles of nutmeg
2 quarts chicken broth
1/2 cup grated Parmesan cheese

Combine egg yolks, bread crumbs, 3 T grated cheese, and nutmeg. Fold egg whites into the mixture. Bring the chicken broth to a boil; drop the egg-cheese-bread crumb mixture one teaspoonful at a time into the boiling broth. Stir constantly with a fork until the eggs set. Serve with the remainder of the grated Parmesan cheese.

SPLIT PEA SOUP

1 lb split peas
1 smoked hambone
1/2 cup chopped carrots
2 celery stalks, diced
2 medium onions, sliced
8 peppercorns

4 whole cloves
8 cups boiling water
3/4 t sugar
1/2 cup half-and-half or thin
   cream
salt and pepper

Wash peas and drain. Place peas with hambone, vegetables, and water in a soup pot. Cover and simmer over low heat until the peas are soft, about 30 minutes, stirring occasionally. Force through a sieve (or use a blender or Cuisinart). Add enough cream to give the desired consistency. Add sugar, salt and pepper. Reheat and serve. Makes 6 generous servings.

NOTE: Can replace hambone with 4 strips of bacon. Fry the bacon in an iron skillet, add onions, carrot, and celery; sauté briefly. Then add peas, water, bacon, and vegetables to the soup pot.

LENTIL SOUP: Substitute 2 cups lentils for split peas and 3 T vinegar plus 1/2 t dry mustard in place of the cream.

BLACK BEAN SOUP: Substitute 2 cups black beans for split peas. Soak beans 12 hours; then cook 1-1/2 to 2 hours. Use 1/4 cup sherry for the cream. Serve with slices of lemon and hard-boiled eggs.

CREAM OF BROCCOLI or CAULIFLOWER SOUP

1 large cauliflower or broccoli cut up into small pieces and florets
1/4 cup butter
2 T chopped onion
3 celery ribs, minced
1/4 cup flour

4 cups veal or chicken stock
2 cups scalded milk or cream
A grating of nutmeg
Salt
Paprika
Grated cheese

Steam the cauliflower or broccoli until tender. Reserve 1 cup of the water and 1/3 of the florets. Put the remainder of the vegetable in a blender or Cuisinart. Sauté onions and celery ribs in the butter until tender Stir in 1/4 cup flour.

Bring the stock to the boiling point and add the blended vegetables and sautéed onion/celery mixture. Add the scalded milk, a grating of nutmeg, salt, and paprika. Garnish with grated cheese. Makes 5-6 cups.

DAWNE BOND'S NAVY BEAN SOUP

Soak 1/2 cup navy or white beans. Add:

A small piece of ham, a ham-
    bone, or 1/8 lb salt pork
4 cups boiling water

1 bay leaf
3-4 whole black peppercorns
3 whole cloves

Cook soup for 2-1/2 to 3 hours or until the beans are soft. During
the last 30 minutes add:

1 diced carrot
3 ribs of celery with leaves,
    chopped
1/2 sliced onion

1 minced garlic clove*
1/8 t saffron*
1/2 cup fresh mashed potatoes*
1/2 cup sorrel*

The last four starred ingredients are optional but their addition
turns this Navy Bean soup into the famous "United States Senate
Bean Soup."

NOTE: Dawne Diaz Bond's husband, Bill Bond, represented
Long Beach's 39th District in the California State Assembly from
1973-1974.

POTATO SOUP WITH BEEF STOCK

1 cup rich beef stock
1 small onion sliced very fine and softened in 1 T butter or bacon
    drippings
1/2 cup celery tops sliced very fine.
1/2 cup carrots
2 cups potatoes

Cut all the vegetables very fine and let cook in the stock until soft
and the potatoes start to fall apart. Season well with salt and
pepper.

Make a roux with 1/2 T butter, 1/2 T flour, 1 cup whole or skim
milk. When vegetables are soft, stir in the cream sauce and simmer 15-20 minutes.

Before serving add 2-3 drops hot pepper sauce or cayenne pepper
and 1-2 T chopped fresh parsley.

MINESTRA DI PASQUA ("Easter Soup")

1 head escarole (about 1-1/2 lbs)
Salt
1 slice stale bread, crust re-
   moved
1/4 cup milk
1/2 lb ground beef
1 egg

3 quarts chicken broth
1/3 cup quadrattini (or other)
   pasta
2 hard-boiled eggs, sliced thin
1/2 cup freshly grated Parmesan
   cheese

Wash and trim the escarole and cut in half. Cook in boiling salted water for 4 minutes or until just tender. Drain, plunge into ice water, drain, and squeeze dry. [NOTE: Escarole can be steamed for 4-5 minutes as a healthier alternative to boiling it.] Cut into 1/4-in strips and set aside.

Place bread in a bowl and cover with milk. Let soften 10 minutes; then squeeze dry. Combine the bread with the ground beef, egg, and 1 t salt. Make tiny meatballs the size of marbles. This should make 48-50 marbles.

Bring the chicken broth to a boil; add meatballs, and simmer 5 minutes. Add the escarole and pasta and cook another 10 minutes.

Divide the hard-boiled egg slices among the bottoms of wide soup dishes. Ladle on the soup and sprinkle with Parmesan cheese.

Libertario Chiarello age 6 (1914)
Born June 5, 1908 San'Arica, Italy
Died July 15, 2007 Webster, NY
Known to his daughters as "Meinpapa"
Known to the rest of the world as Leo P. Sherrell

Chapter IV

VEGETABLES
& VEGETARIAN DISHES

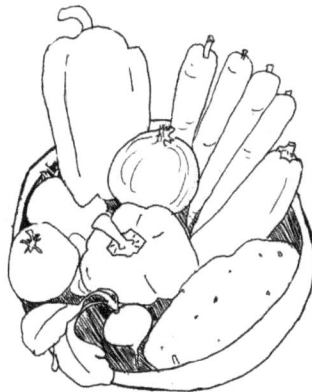

BROCCOLI RABE

Broccoli rabe is also called rapa or rapini ("little rapa"). "Rapa" in Italian means "wild turnip" and rapini refers to young wild turnip greens. They can easily be grown in a Seattle backyard.

Rinse the rapini and cut off the base of stems. Cross crosswise into 2-in lengths and steam for 1-2 minutes or until tender.

Heat 2-3 T olive oil in a large skiller over medium-high heat. Add 2-3 minced cloves of garlic and cook 2-3 minutes. Add the rapini and cook briefly. Season with salt and pepper, a dash of cayenne pepper, hot pepper sauce, or red pepper flakes.

Rapini may also be served with penne or other pasta or with cooked white beans, at which point it becomes "beans & greens."

ROMAN-STYLE SPINACH

1 lb spinach, well washed
1 carrot, shredded
2 T olive oil
2 garlic cloves, minced
2 T raisins (or dried cranberries_
1/4 t salt
1/4 t pepper
1 T toasted pine nuts

Steam spinach until wilted. Heat the olive oil in a heavy skillet, and add the minced garlic and shredded carrot. Cook briefly, until the garlic turns golden. Add the raisins and spinach, cover, and turn off the heat. When ready to serve, stir in the toasted pine nuts.

PEPPERS & EGGPLANT ("Peperoni e Melanzane")

4 T olive oil
1 medium red or yellow onion, cut in half & sliced thin
4 peppers (green or yellow or red), cut into rings
2 medium eggplants: cut in half, then 1 in slices
2 small zucchini: cut in half, then 1 in slices
1/2 lb sliced mushrooms
1 cup stewed tomatoes (without skins)

Pour olive oil in a heavy-bottomed casserole. Add in layers first the onions, then peppers, eggplants, and zucchini. Add the tomatoes and sprinkle with salt and pepper. Do not mix.

Cover the casserole and place it on medium heat. Simmer for 20 minutes without mixing. Then mix thoroughly and taste for salt and pepper. Simmer for 15 minutes more, uncovered, stirring every so often with a wooden spoon.

This dish may accompany boiled or roasted meat. Do not use it with main dishes that have a tomato sauce.

EGGPLANT PARMIGIANA

1 large or 2 medium eggplants,
    cut in 1/2-in slices
1 t salt
1 medium onion, chopped
1-2 cloves garlic, finely chopped
1 can Italian tomatoes,
    undrained
1/2 t basil, crumbled

1/2 t oregano, crumbled
1 t salt
1/4 t pepper
2 eggs
3/4 cup grated Parmesan
1/2 lb sliced mozzarella cheese
Olive oil as needed

Heat oven to 350°F. Heat 2 T olive oil in a heavy saucepan. Sauté onion and garlic 5 minutes. Add tomatoes, basil, oregano, salt, and pepper. Cover; simmer 20 minutes. Meanwhile, combine eggs and flour in a small bowl and beat until smooth. Dip eggplant slices in egg mixture; drain slightly. Sauté in hot oil on both sides, using about 2 T oil at a time. Place a single layer of eggplant in a shallow 2-quart baking dish. Cover with half the tomato sauce, half the Parmesan cheese, and half the mozzarella. Repeat with a second layer. Sprinkle with remaining Parmesan. Bake 25 minutes or until thoroughly heated. Makes 6-8 servings.

ZUCCHINI FRITTATA

1 medium zucchini, sliced
1 medium tomato, sliced
1/4 onion, minced
6-8 fresh basil leaves cut into strips
1 t oregano
1/2 t salt
dash of fresh grated pepper
1/2 cup cottage cheese or ricotta cheese
5 T grated Parmesan cheese
2 T olive oil
5 eggs

Beat eggs lightly with salt, pepper, basil and oregano. Stir in cottage cheese and half the Parmesan. Set aside. Sauté the zucchini and onion in oil in a heavy iron skillet until they are lightly browned. Pour in the egg mixture, place tomato slices on top, and sprinkle with remaining Parmesan cheese. Cook over medium heat until eggs are set on the bottom of the pan, about 10 minutes; then place skillet under the broiler until lightly brown. Cut into wedges and serve hot.

GATTO DI PATATE ALLA CALABRESE
("Potato Cake of Calabria")

1 cup mashed potatoes
1 cup flour
3 t baking powder
A few parsley sprigs, finely chopped
1/2 cup grated Parmesan cheese
2 eggs, slightly beaten
Salt and pepper to taste
Cooking oil

Mix together all the ingredients except the oil. Shape into 3-in long rolls about 1-in in diameter. Heat the oil in a heavy skillet and fry the potato cakes in 1-in of hot oil until golden brown. Serve hot, as a vegetable, or as a bread. Makes 6-8 servings.

RISOTTO MILANESE

2 T extra-virgin olive oil
2-1/2 T unsalted butter
1 cup Arborio rice
1 medium onion, chopped
1-2 cloves garlic, pressed

3-1/2 cups chicken stock
1/2 t saffron
3 T Madeira, Marsala or sherry
1/2 cup grated Parmesan cheese

Risotto involves cooking the rice in stages. Heat olive oil and 2 T butter in heavy iron skillet. Add rice and cook until it turns pale yellow. Add onion and garlic; cook over low heat for 2 minutes. Add 1 cup chicken stock and cook, covered, for 15 minutes or until liquid is absorbed. Add saffron, Madeira, and remaining stock and stir. Cover and cook slowly until all the liquid is absorbed. Just before serving, add remaining butter and cheese and toss slightly. Serve at once as a separate course or with a green salad. Yield: 4 servings.

NOTE #1: Tomato sauce, mushrooms, giblets, shrimp, clams, prawns, sausages, truffles, herbs and wine can all be added to embellish the risotto.

NOTE #2: PROSCIUTTO & ASPARAGUS variation: Substitute 1 cup dry white wine for 1 cup of chicken stock. Cut 1 bunch asparagus into 1/4-in slices. When the risotto has achieved the desired consistency, add asparagus pieces (saving some for a garnish), 1/4 lb prosciutto cut into thin strips, and 1/4 cup unsalted butter. Add the grated Parmesan and beat vigorously. Serve, garnishing each plate with 3 asparagus bits.
—Susan Sherrell, November 17, 2009

BEANS & GREENS

1 cup cleaned escarole	2 pinches pepper
1 cup cleaned broccoli rabe	1 oz. prosciutto
2 T olive oil	1 oz. bacon
6-8 cloves garlic	2 cups cooked cannelloni beans
2 pinches salt	1/4 cup grated Parmesan

Steam greens until wilted and set aside. In a heavy skillet, heat the olive oil until hot. Add garlic, salt, pepper, prosciutto and bacon and sauté. Add wilted greens and cooked cannelloni beans and heat for about 10 minutes. Sprinkle with grated Parmesan and serve. Makes 4 servings.

—Mildred Spinoza

NOTE: In Argentina I used *jamón crudo* in place of the prosciutto and bacon, and *poroto payar* in place of the cannelloni beans. The *poroto payar* were beautiful, fresh, red-and-white beans. I brought a small pot of water to a boil and cooked the fresh beans for 10 minutes. Utterly *fantástico*.

—GC, January 17 and 26, 2010

ROASTED POTATOES WITH ONIONS

2-1/2 lb (5 medium) potatoes)
1 medium onion cut into
    wedges
5 sprigs thyme, oregano or
    rosemary

2 bay leaves
3/4 cup extra-virgin olive oil
salt
fresh ground black pepper

Preheat oven to 450° F. Scrub potatoes, leaving skins on. Cut each potato in half crosswise; then cut each half into 8 wedges. Rinse in cold water and pat dry. Place potatoes, onion, and herbs in a large roasting pan. Pour olive oil over and ross to coat. Roast in hot oven 35-40 minutes or until browned on outside and tender within, turning occasionally. NOTE: Use a large enough pan for a single layer of potatoes. Makes 6 servings.

POTATO CASSEROLE

6-8 cups mashed potatoes
1/3 cup grated Parmesan cheese
1/3 cup dried bread crumbs
8 eggs, beaten
1/3 cup chopped green olives
1 small onion, chopped

2-4 oz sharp Cheddar cheese,
    shredded
3-4 oz salami or pepperoni, diced
Parsley, chopped
Red pepper, chopped small
Salt, fresh ground black pepper

Oil a 9x13 Pyrex pan and set aside. Combine ingredients and place in pan. Bake at 350° for 30 minutes. Makes 6-8 servings.

GREEK ZUCCHINI & PASTA

3 cups zucchini cut into 1/2-in
    slices
1/2 cup chopped onion
1/4 cup olive oil
2 cups freshed chopped toma-
    toes
2 T fresh chopped mind

2 T fresh chopped dill
3/4 t salt
1/8 t fresh grated pepper
1/2 cup plain yoghurt
8 oz dried pasta, cooked &
    drained
1/4 lb crumbled feta cheese

Sauté the onion and zucchini in a large skillet about 5 minutes or until translucent. Add tomatoes, mint, dill, salt and pepper, and cover, simmering for 15 minutes. Stir in the yoghurt and cook another 3 minutes. Serve over the pasta and sprinkle with the crumbled feta cheese. Makes 6 servings.

ROASTED VEGETABLES

3 large red bell peppers
2 medium zucchini
2 medium yellow-neck squash
1 eggplant
1 large sweet onion
1-2 Portobello mushrooms

1 Garnet sweet potato
1/2 cup extra-virgin olive oil
1 t dried thyme
1/2 t salt
1/4 t pepper
Juice of 1/2 lemon

Cut vegetables into interesting shapes, as all cut into long thin spears; or all into rounds and rings. Grease a large cookie sheet and lay the vegetables on it. Drizzle them with the mixture of olive oil, thyme, salt and pepper. Bake in a hot oven (350°-400° F), setting a timer for 25 minutes. Turn them all over; you will see there will be brown on the bottom. Set timer for another 20 minutes and check them again. If some vegetables appear to be cooking faster than others, set those aside on a plate. When vegetables are done, place on a serving plate and drizzle with the lemon juice.

SWEET & SOUR RED CABBAGE

1 onion, chopped
3 T butter
9 cups shredded red cabbage
1 large tart apple, diced
1/2 cup cider vinegar

1 cup water
3 T brown sugar
1 T caraway seeds
1-1/4 t salt
1/4 t pepper

Cook onion in butter for 5 minutes. Add cabbage; cover and cook for 5 more minutes. Add remaining ingredients, cover, and simmer or bake for 1 hour at 325°. Makes about 6 servings.

PASTA E FAGIOLI ("Pasta Fazool")

1/4 cup olive oil
1 minced clove garlic
1 cup or more diced onion
1 cup or more diced celery
1/2 cup diced carrots
1 16-oz canned plum tomatos
1/2 t oregano
1/2 t fresh ground black pepper

1/4 t crushed red pepper
1 cup dried cannelloni (white) beans
1/2 cup uncooked ditalini or other small pasta; cooked separately
1 cup green vegetables (escarole, zucchini, broccoli, etc)

Soak beans for 12 hours; drain, and transfer to a heavy saucepan. Add water to cover about 1 inch and bring to a boil over medium heat. Reduce heat to low and simmer very gently under beans are tender and most of the liquid has been absorbed, about 1-1/2 hours.

Heat oil. Add garlic and onion and sauté a few minutes. Add celery and carrots; sauté a few more minutes. Add tomato and spices and cook together about 10 minutes. Add beans and 1 can water; bring to a boil. Cook on low heat for about 1 hour. Meanwhile cook pasta in salted (to taste) water. Drain and add to bean mixture, with vegetables, if desired, and cook together for an additional 15-30 minutes.

For a soupier soup, use some of the water drained from the pasta. This will make about 3 quarts of soup or 9 good-sized servings. For a complete meal in one dish, add sliced cooked Italian sausage.

—FCM, June 29, 1997

PASTA WITH ROASTED RED PEPPER TOMATO SAUCE

2 T olive oil
1 medium onion, chopped
1-2 cloves garlic, minced
1 28-oz can whole tomatoes,
   drained and chopped
1 red pepper, roasted and cut
   into strips

3/4 cup chicken broth
1 t dried basil
1 t dried oregano
1 lb dried farfalle (bow-tie)
   pasta
2 T grated Parmesan or
   Romano cheese

Heat olive oil in heavy skillet over medium heat; add onion and garlic
and cook 5 minutes. Add tomatoes, red pepper, broth, and herbs.
Heat to boiling, then reduce heat and simmer 10 minutes, uncovered.
In Cuisinart or blender, process 1/2 the tomato sauce mixture until
smooth; return to skillet with remaining sauce.

Meanwhile cook pasta according to package directions. Toss hot pasta
and sauce together and sprinkle with Parmesan cheese. Makes about
10 servings of 1 cup each.

MARINARA SAUCE

4 T olive oil	4 lbs (6 cups) fresh tomatoes
2 onions chopped	Oregano, basil, thyme
2 minced garlic cloves	

Begin by cutting up the fresh tomatoes and placing in a blender (may need to do this in stages). Have ready a large saucepan, add the blended tomatoes to the saucepan; bring contents to a boil and then turn down heat, simmering until all the foam has condensed and sauce is as thick as you like it.

Heat olive oil and add onions and garlic, stirring until golden. Add fresh herbs to taste. Then add unflavored tomato sauce and let simmer for 1-2 hours on low heat. This sauce will "set up" and be better the next day.

POLENTA (CORN MEAL MUSH)

Mix 1 cup corn meal with 1 cup cold water. Bring 2 more cups of water plus 1 teaspoon salt to a boil in a saucepan, and add the corn meal and cold water mixture. Stir vigorously for 2-3 minutes. Corn meal will thicken up right away. When thick, pour onto a large plate or platter and let cool. Serves 6-8.

NOTE: 2-3 bouillon cubes can be added to the boiling water above.

PESTO

Basic approach, equipment and ingredients:

1 7-cup Cuisinart or blender	1 cube unsalted butter
1-2 large clean dishtowels	1/2 lb Parmesan cheese
3-4 home-grown basil plants	1 cup olive oil
2 cups pine nuts or walnuts	2-3 large cloves garlic

Wash 6-12 plastic containers (2-1/2" diameter) and lids, and 2 rubber spatulas (one with narrow blade) in hot soapy water. Rinse. Bring a kettle of water to a boil. Set the spatula blades in the containers and add boiling water, lightly setting the lids on top. Let sterilize for 10-15 minutes. Drain and place on a clean dishtowel. Meanwhile, strip leaves/flowers off basil plants and place in large bowl. Fill with cold water; wash the leaves; drain in a colander. There should be no mud, dirt, or dust from the garden on them. Spread them on a clean dishtowel; roll up and press dry. (The dishtowel may turn green, but this will wash out.) The leaves should not be wet. Add leaves and olive oil to the blender or Cuisinart and blend to a paste. Cut the Parmesan into small chunks before adding it to the mixture. Blend again. Add the pine nuts or walnuts and butter, cut into small chunks. When the mixture is as you want it, start filling the containers, using the narrow-bladed spatula to make sure there are no air holes in the mixture. Then cap the containers and, when cool, place in the refrigerator of freezer.

NOTE: Do the recipe in thirds, because the blender may not be able to handle the entire mixture. The basil leaves must be added with oil; otherwise the leaves will line the glass and won't turn into a paste. Don't worry about proportions; in pesto, nothing need be exact. Romano or Asiego cheese is acceptable in lieu of Parmesan.

LASAGNA

Clean the entire kitchen so that it is spotless. Put on some opera or Italian folk-songs.

Assemble:
1 large black iron skillet or Dutch oven (two, for double recipe)
Extra-virgin olive oil
1 lg. can Contadina tomato puree or 1 quart tomato sauce
1 sm. can Contadina tomato paste
1 very large onion
3 plump cloves garlic
Herbs: 1 T oregano and/or basil
Spices: 1 t "4-Spice Powder": cinnamon, nutmeg, allspice, cloves
Brown sugar
1 plump large lemon
Some leftover not-too-bad wine (red or white)
1/2 lb fresh white mushrooms
1 box lasagna noodles
1 lb. fresh ricotta cheese
1 lb. fresh mozzarella cheese

Step #1: Put iron pot on high-medium heat. Add olive oil. Chop onion finely, mince garlic, and add to pot. Add fresh herbs (minced or chopped). Stir with wooden spoon until onions are translucent. Add tomato paste and stir some more.

Step #2: Add tomato puree. Add wine and lemon juice with water to make 1 cup. Slice mushrooms to make little umbrellas and add to mixture. Add 2 T brown sugar. Add 1 t mixture of ground cinnamon, allspice, and nutmeg.

Step #3: Turn down heat to low. Cover, using large plate if you have no lid. Let cook for 3-4 hours . (Stir every hour or so). Let sit over night (in refrigerator)

Step #4 (next day): Find large glass or metal rectangular pan slightly longer than the lasagna noodles . Bring large pot of water to boil with some salt and 1 T. oil, add 10 lasagna noodles, 3 at a time, slowly. Cook about 12 minutes, test one noodle. Should be done but very slightly chewy (but not too chewy)

Assembling the lasagna:
Oil bottom of lasagna pan.
Add a spoonful of sauce and cover bottom of pan with it.
Arrange 3 cooked lasagna noodles side by side on the bottom.
Take your cheese and cut them up into 3 portions (one for each
    layer).
Dab 1/3 the mozzarella and ricotta on layer number 1, and then
    add sauce.
Add 3 more lasagna noodles side by side. Repeat above step.
Add 3 more lasagna noodles side by side. (The extra noodle is in
    case one breaks). Repeat above step.
Cover dish with aluminum foil and place in 300 oven.
Bake 1 hour or longer.

First day it will be runny. Subsequent days (if there are subsequent days) it will start to dry out (which is good, some think).

Serve with broccoli rabe (page 38).

Alba Chiarello Diaz age 15 (1930)
Born June 15, 1915 Albany, NY
Died 2008 Long Beach, CA

Chapter V

MAIN COURSES

PIZZA FOR FOUR

Dough:
1 pkg dry yeast
1 cup water at 105° F

3 cups flour
1 t salt
1 T olive oil

Sauce:
3 T olive oil
1 sliced onion
1 large minced garlic clove

1 28-oz can tomato puree
1 cup water
1 t each oregano and basil
Salt, pepper, parsley to taste

Dissolve yeast in water; add flour and salt and knead thoroughly for about 15 minutes. Add olive oil and knead until smooth. Cover in warm place for about 3 hours or until double in bulk.
Brown onion and garlic in the olive oil; add tomato puree, water, herbs and salt and pepper. Simmer 1/2 hour or more.

Spread 1/2 the dough on a well-oiled cookie sheet or pizza pan. Pour over a little sauce and add grated cheese, mozzarella cheese, anchovies, mushrooms, peppers, peperoni. Cover with more sauce. Bake in a *very* hot oven (550° F) for 10 minutes; then reduce heat to 350° F for another 10 minutes. Check frequently.

Use remainder of dough for rolls, bread sticks (page 23), or a second pizza.

NOTE: Add toppings as you wish: anchovies; black olives; sliced hot sausage; capers; various other cheeses.

CHICKEN CACCIATORE

1-1/4 lbs boneless, skinless
    chicken breasts or thighs
3 T extra-virgin olive oil
Coarse salt & pepper to taste
1/2 t crushed red pepper flakes
3 cloves garlic, minced
1 medium onion, chopped
3 Portobello mushroom caps,
    thinly sliced
1 cup dry red wine or beef stock

1 28-oz can crushed tomatoes
Handful chopped Italian parsley
Handful chopped basil, rosemary
1 lb rigatoni or other pasta, cooked al dente
Grated Romano or Parmesan cheese

Chop chicken into bite size pieces and brown on all sides over medium high heat, using 1 T olive oil. Remove from heat and set aside. Add remaining olive oil, garlic, onion, and crushed red pepper flakes to the pan; sauté briefly; then add mushrooms. Cook until mushrooms are dark and tender and have given their juices—5-7 minutes. Add wine or stock to the pan and reduce the liquid for 1-2 minutes; then add tomatoes and herbs. Slide chicken back into pan and stir in fresh chopped parsley; simmer 25 minutes. Spoon over platefuls of cooked rigatoni and top with grated cheese. Serve with green salad and crusty bread. Serves 4.

CHICKEN LIVERS WITH SAGE

1 lb chicken livers, each liver cut into 2 or 3 pieces
1/4 cup butter
1/4 t salt
1/8 t fresh ground pepper
1 t chopped fresh sage leaves

2 slices prosciutto or bacon, cut in slivers
4 slices bread, cut into triangles and fried in butter
1/2 cup Marsala or sherry
1 T butter

Melt 1/4 cup butter in a shallow pan. Add the chicken livers, salt, pepper, sage, and prosciutto and cook about 5 minutes. Remove livers from pan and place on warm serving dish, on the fried bread triangles. Add wine to pan juices, mix well, and cook 3 minutes. Add 1 T butter, mix well, and pour over livers and fried bread. Serves 4.

CHICKEN with DUMPLINGS

1 whole cut-up chicken
1-1/2 cups flour
1 T butter
1-1/2 t baking powder
1 t salt

Mace or nutmeg
1/2 onion, minced
2 eggs, beaten
1/2 cup milk, or more

Simmer a whole chicken until cooked. Remove chicken and set aside.

Mix together flour, baking powder, salt and spices, onion, eggs and milk. Drop by tablespoonfuls into the hot chicken broth, cover tightly, and simmer for 15 minutes. Remove cover and serve at once.

ALBA'S CHAMPAGNE CHICKEN

4 chicken breasts
1 cup flour
salt & pepper
1/2 cup sliced mushrooms

1/2 cup butter
1 cup cream or milk
1/2 cup champagne or white
   wine

Pound chicken breasts between 2 sheets of waxed paper to flatten.
Brown breasts in butter; add mushrooms; cover and cook 10 minutes. Add cream or milk; cover and cook 10 more minutes. Remove chicken to a warm platter. Add wine to sauce and bring to a
bubble; turn off immediately. Serve with pasta, linguine, or rice.
May be made a day ahead of time and re-warmed in a microwave.
Alba's favorite dish for company.

FLORA'S VEAL AND PEPPERS

2 lbs boneless veal, cubed
2 red or green bell peppers
1 large onion, chopped
3 cloves garlic, minced
2 cups homemade tomato sauce

1/2 cup red wine
Oregano, basil, hot red pepper
    (dried and crushed), black
    pepper, salt to taste

Quarter peppers and remove white membrane and seeds. Place on a cookie sheet and roast in a 450° F oven or under an electric broiler, checking frequently. Remove as soon as skins are slightly charred (5-10 minutes depending on heat); cut into strips, set aside.

Pat veal cubes dry and brown in hot olive oil. Remove and set aside; add chopped onion and herbs. When onions are golden, add the tomato sauce and wine. (A splash of pomegranate syrup—maybe 1-2 tablespoons—can be a nice addition at this point.) Cook for 2 hours over very low heat, stirring every 15-20 minutes.

When everything is ready, cut the roasted peppers into chunks about the size of the meat, and combine with the tomato sauce, meat, and peppers. Reheat if necessary, and serve with rice, pasta, or polenta.

—FCM, June 4, 1999

VEAL SCALOPPINE MARSALA

1 lb boneless veal round, sliced
   1/4-in thick, pounded thin
   for scaloppini
1/2 t salt
1/4 t fresh ground black pepper
1/2 cup flour
2 T butter
3-4 large garlic cloves, sliced

1 cup Marsala or dry red wine
1/2 cup sliced mushrooms
1 T lemon juice
1 t grated lemon rind
1/4 cup loosely packed chopped
   fresh parsley leaves

Mix salt and pepper into flour; coat veal with flour mixture . Brown garlic in butter over medium high heat in a large skillet; when golden brown, remove and set aside. Brown veal in pan; when seared, remove and keep warm. Add mushrooms, lemon juice, lemon rind, and wine to the pan and cook 2-3 minutes, stirring to loosen brown bits. Pour over veal and sprinkle with parsley. Serves 4.

MEINPAPA'S MARINATED STEAKS

Place 4 rib-eye or sirloin steaks in a 9x13 Pyrex baking dish and use just enough marinade to cover the meat. Put in the refrigerator, preferably the day before, to let the vinegar do the tenderizing.

Marinade: The main ingredient is 1/2 cup vinegar (any vinegar will do; Pa uses cider vinegar; Donaldo uses Balsamic); then enough water to cover the steaks, and whatever spices are on hand—pepper, oregano, basil, grated onion, and/or garlic.

—Meinpapa, June 22, 1999
(updated Don Sherrell December 1, 2009)

BARBEQUED HAMBURGERS

1-1/2 lb hamburger	1/4 cup ketchup
3 T grated onion	1/2 t chili powder
1/3 cup corn flakes	1/2 cup water
3/4 t salt	dash of Tabasco
1/4 t pepper	

Mix and shape into 7-8 patties. Brown in a heavy skillet on both sides. Blend ketchup, chili powder, water and Tabasco and pour over the meat patties. Cover and cook slowly, about 1 hour. Can be frozen or reheated.

SAUERBRATEN

1-1/4 lb boneless beef sirloin tip
Oil or butter
3 cups baby carrots
1-1/2 cups pearl onions (classic)
   or use sliced fresh onion
1/4 cup raisins
1/2 cup water
1/2 cup red wine vinegar

1 T honey or brown sugar
1/2 t salt
1/2 t dry mustard
1 clove garlic, minced
1/4 t ground cloves
5 crushed gingersnap cookies
   (classic, but optional)

Heat oil or butter in a large skillet and brown the garlic, then brown roast on all sides; then set all aside.

Place beef, carrots, pearl onions and raisins in a slow cooker. Combine water, vinegar, honey, salt, mustard, pepper and cloves in a large bowl and mix well. Pour over the meat and vegetables. Cover and cook on low 4-6 hours or until internal temperature of roast reaches 145° F when tested with a meat thermometer inserted into the thickest part of the roast. Transfer roast to a cutting board and cover with foil, letting stand 10-15 minutes. Internal temperature will continue to rise during this time. Remove vegetables with a slotted spoon and place in bowl; cover to keep warm. Stir crushed gingersnaps into sauce mixture in slow cooker. Cover and cook on high 10-15 minutes or until sauce thickens. Serve meat and vegetables with sauce. Makes 5 servings.

CHILI

1 lb ground beef	3-4 T chili powder
Oil or shortening	1/2 t ground black pepper
1/2 cup green pepper, chopped	1/2 t crushed red pepper
1/2 cup onion, chopped	1 cup canned or fresh tomatoes
1/4 cup fresh parsley, chopped	3 cups tomato sauce
1 t salt	2 cups cooked red kidney beans
1 t oregano	1/4 lb sliced black olives
1 T sugar	Grated yellow cheese

Heat skillet and melt a little suet or 1 tablespoon shortening. Add ground meat and break up into small pieces. Brown slightly. Add onion, pepper, and parsley; stir until onion and pepper are soft. Add tomatoes and cook over a high flame until most of the juice boils away. Then add the seasonings, stirring until well mixed. Add tomato sauce, one can at a time. Cook over a low flame for 20 -30 minutes. Heat kidney beans with a few tablespoons of chili mixture.

Make polenta (page 52) and pour half the cooked polenta into a 2-quart serving bowl. Add the chili, top with sliced olives, and add remainder of the polenta. Top with grated cheese and bake in a hot oven (350° F) until the cheese is browned. Serves 4.

TAMALE PIE

1 cup chopped onions
1 large green pepper, coarsely chopped
1 clove garlic, minced
1 T oil
1 lb lean ground beef (95 % lean)
1 cup thick tomato sauce
1/2 cup shredded Monterey Jack cheese
1 T minced jalapeño pepper
2 t chili powder
1 cup cornmeal

Sauté onions, green pepper and garlic. Add beef and cook until browned; drain excess fat. Stir in ketchup/thick tomato sauce, jalapeño pepper and chili powder; heat to boiling.

Prepare polenta by mixing the corn meal with cold water, then adding to 3 cups salted boiling water. When the batter thickens, spoon around the edges of an 8 inch baking dish. Carefully spoon meat mixture into center of dish and bake at 375° F for 29 minutes. Top mixture with cheese and bake an additional 5 minutes. Remove from oven and let stand for 5 minutes before serving. Serves 4. Enjoy.

—Meinpapa, June 22, 1999

FLORA'S CORNED BEEF

One corned beef about 2-3 lbs
3 cloves garlic, minced
1 medium onion, quartered
1 bay leaf

2 cloves
1 carrot, quartered
Black peppercorns

Rinse corned beef under cold running water and place in a large pot with a heavy bottom, fatty side up. Arrange vegetables and seasonings around the corned beef, and cover everything with cold water. Bring pot to a boil, then turn heat way down, and let the corned beef simmer for about 2 hours. Do not overcook! Remove from pot, slice, and serve at once. Alternatively the corned beef can be refrigerated and eaten later.

—FCM, November 3, 1997

PORK CHOPS & SAUERKRAUT

1 lb pork chops or ribs
1-2 medium onions, sliced
2-4 large cloves garlic
1 small can sauerkraut

1 cup applesauce
1/2 t pepper
1 t caraway or anise seed
1 cup water or beer

Brown pork chops in 1 T oil in a heavy skillet. Add onions and garlic and cook 2 minutes. Rinse sauerkraut well and add it to the skillet with the remaining ingredients. Cover and cook on low heat 1 to 1-1/2 hour.

Pa's comments. *"I use my heavy cast iron kettle. Depending on the amount of kraut to be cooked, I dice 1-2 cooking onions and 1-2 garlic cloves in a small amount of oil. If the pork has very little fat, I dice up a small piece of salt pork and brown that in the pan before I add the onions and the garlic. While the onions and garlic are browning, I drain the water from the kraut and add to the kettle, adding just enough water or, preferably, beer to cover, and adding the caraway seed. Set the pot over a very low flame and let it simmer for a couple of hours. Check the amount of liquid and add more as needed, The sauerkraut left over is even better the next day when reheated BUT NOT BURNED!"*

—Meinpapa [date not recorded]

NOTE: Excellent served with simple steamed or boiled potatoes.

FLORA'S LAMB STEW

1/4 cup butter
2 medium onions, thinly sliced
Chopped celery leaves, parsley, thyme, rosemary
1 bay leaf
3 lbs lamb shoulder, cubed
1 cup boiling water
1 8-oz can tomato sauce
1 16-oz can green beans
Liquid drained from beans

1 t salt
1/2 t pepper
1 cup celery, sliced
4 carrots cut in 1-in slices
1/4 cup cold water
1 T flour
Fresh chopped parsley, bay
  leaf
1/2 cup mushrooms (optional)
1 cup sour cream (optional)

Heat oil and sauté lamb until browned. Remove and add onions, browning slightly, then add herbs to taste. Add 1 cup water, toma-toes, bean liquid, and simmer covered for 1 hour. Add vegetables. Mix water and flour to make a roux and add to sauce. Add the beans. Optional: 1 cup sour cream and 1/2 cup sliced mushrooms.

Seeing Pa Off 1949
Flora Chiarello Menges, Sesto Chiarello, A. Biagio Chiarello
After Lucia dies, il Notaro sails back to Italy to find a second wife.

Chapter VI

COOKIES

PIZZELLE

6 eggs
1 cup sugar
1 cup melted butter
1 t anise oil or 1 T anise seeds or
    2 t anise extract
2 t vanilla

2 cups flour
2 T baking powder
1/2 t salt
Juice and grated rind of 1 orange
    and 1 lemon

Beat eggs and sugar until they are light and foamy. Add the melted butter a little at a time. Add the anise (seeds, extract, or oil), along with the vanilla, and grated orange and lemon rinds and juice. Gradually add the flour until a light dough is formed—light enough to drop onto the pizzelle iron with a spoon. You may have a little bit of flour left over. Batter can be refrigerated and used at a later time, but best used within 24 hours and has come to room temperature.

Two Vitantonio pizzelle irons are pictured below. These are electric, but the original pizzelle irons had very long handles and were held over a stove.

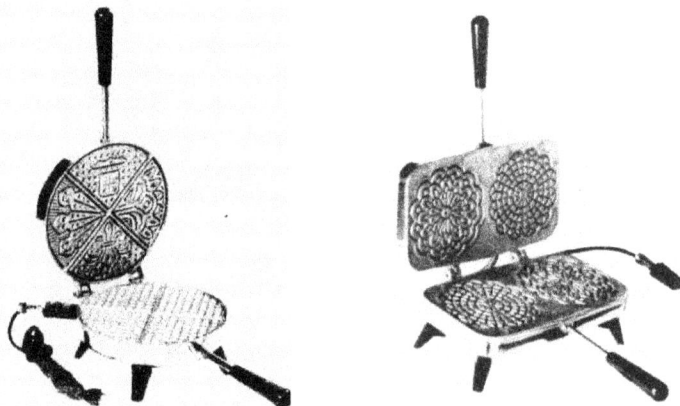

BISCOTTI AL'ANICI ("Anise Biscuits")

1 lb sifted flour
1 t baking powder
1/2 t salt
1/2 cup sugar

6 eggs
1-1/2 t anise extract
1/2 lb unsalted butter

Beat eggs; add sugar; blend thoroughly. Mix together flour, baking powder, and salt. Add softened butter and anise and mix well.

On large greased cookie sheets, shape dough into long loaves 5-in wide and 3/4-in thick, keeping dough at least 2-in away from sides of pan. Make one loaf for each pan. Bake at 350° F for 20 minutes or until light brown. Remove from oven and cut diagonally into 1-in wide slices.

TARALLINI

4 cups flour
1 T baking powder
1/2 t salt
4 eggs
1/2 cup unsalted butter
1/2 cup milk
1 cup sugar
1-1/2 t grated orange rind

Icing:
3 cups confectioners sugar
Grated rind of 1 orange
Water
Colored sprinkles or nonpareils
  (optional)

Line 2 cookie sheets with parchment paper, and preheat the oven to 350° F. Mix flour and baking powder. In a separate bowl, whisk the eggs; then add sugar, melted butter and flavorings. Stir until the wet ingredients are well blended. Fold the dry ingredients into the wet and mix well. Turn out on a floured board and knead gently. Divide the dough into about 30 equal pieces. Roll each piece by hand into a 5 inch rope; then wrap one end over the other to make a bow (see diagram). Place the cookies on baking sheets and bake at 350°F for 15 minutes, until lightly browned. Cool to room temperature.

Icing: Mix confectioners sugar and lemon juice in a bowl. Slowly add a little water until you have the consistency you want. Pick up each cookie, and dip it halfway into the icing. Let the excess drip off, then place cookies on a rack or the paper you used to cook them on. If using colored sprinkles, add them while the icing is still wet. Let the cookies dry completely; then store them in an airtight container.

FORMING TARALLINI:

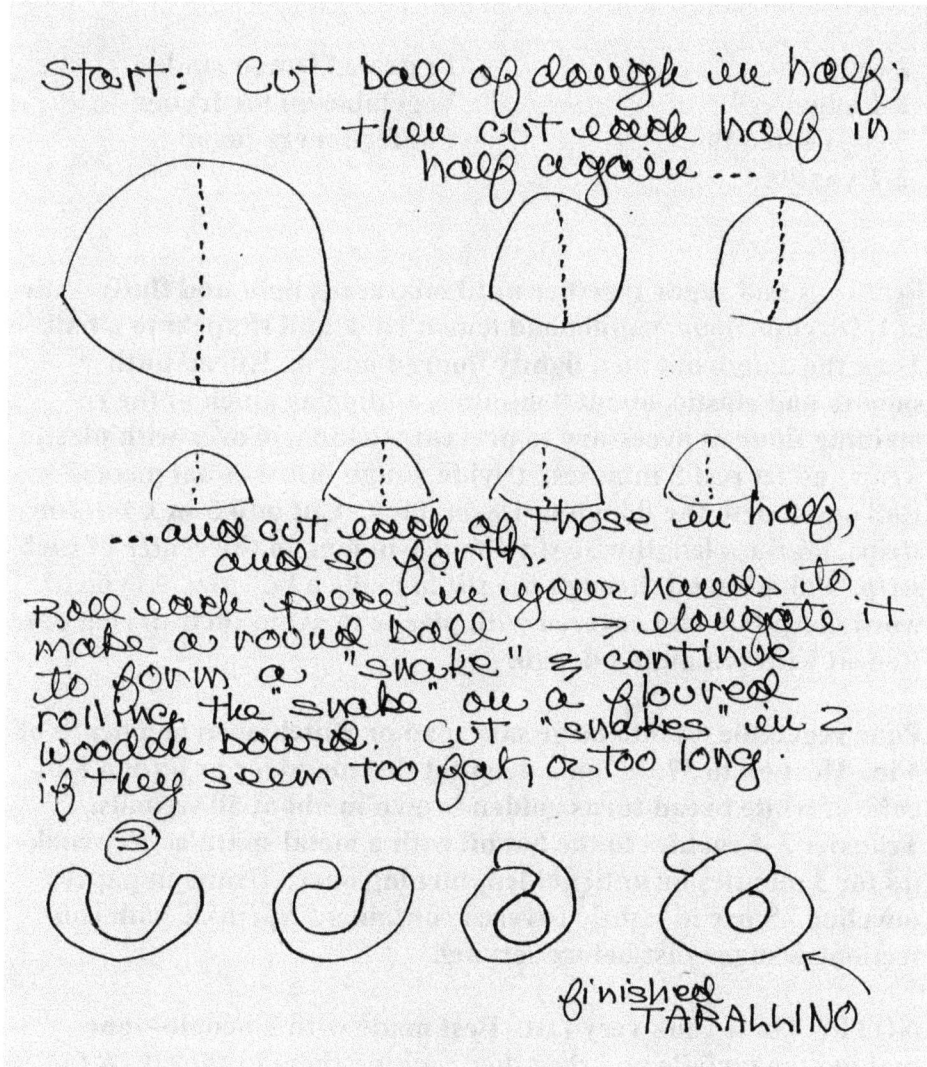

Start: Cut ball of dough in half; then cut each half in half again...

...and cut each of those in half, and so forth.

Ball each piece in your hands to make a round ball —→ elongate it to form a "snake" & continue rolling the "snake" on a floured wooden board. Cut "snakes" in 2 if they seem too fat, or too long.

③

finished TARALLINO

—Diagram by GC, Spring 2010

FARFALLE (Bow-tie Cookies)

2 eggs
2 T sugar
2 cups sifted flour
2 T vanilla

1 t grated lemon rind
Vegetable oil for frying
Confectioners sugar

Beat eggs and sugar together until mixture is light and fluffy. Stir in 1-1/2 cups flour, vanilla and lemon rind, and shape into a ball. Turn the dough out on a lightly floured board. Knead until smooth and elastic, about 8 minutes, adding as much of the remaining flour as necessary to prevent sticking. Cover with plastic wrap and let rest 5 minutes. Divide dough into 4 equal pieces. Roll one-fourth the dough to 1/8-in thick. Cut into 5-in x 1-1/2-in strips. Make a lengthwise slit about 1-in long in the center of each strip. Pull one end through the slit to make a bow tie. As you work, keep bow ties covered with plastic to avoid their drying out. Repeat with remaining dough.

Pour vegetable oil into large saucepan or Dutch oven to a depth of 4 in. Heat oil to 375° F on a deep-fat thermometer or until a 1-in cube of white bread turns golden brown in about 50 seconds. Transfer 3-4 cookies to the hot oil with a metal spatula. Fry cookies for 3 minutes or until golden, turning once. Drain on paper toweling. Store in tightly covered container. Sprinkle with confectioners sugar just before serving.

NOTE: These cook very fast. Best made with 2 people—one making the farfalle and the other cooking them in the oil. A favorite of Flora's mother, Lucia Longo Chiarello.

THIMBLE COOKIES

1 cup butter
1/2 cup sugar
2 egg yolks, beaten
1/2 t salt
3 cups flour
1 t vanilla

2 egg whites beaten slightly
1-1/2 cups chopped walnuts
1 silver thimble
Jelly, jam, or marmalade
Confectioners sugar

Blend together butter, sugar, egg yolks and vanilla; add to flour and salt mixture. Chill dough. Roll bits of dough into walnut-sized balls. Dip in beaten egg whites, then in chopped nuts. Dip thimble in flour and dent centers of the cookies. Place on greased cookie sheets, and bake at 375 ° F for 5 minutes. Dent cookie centers again and return to oven for another 10-12 minutes. Fill centers with jelly or jam. Dust with confectioners sugar.

CHOCOLATE ALMOND DROPS

3 eggs
1/4 t salt
1-1/2 cup sugar
1/2 cup sifted flour

1-1/2 cup almonds, blanched,
    then toasted and ground fine
1 cup chocolate chips ground
    fine
1-1/2 t vanilla

Beat eggs, gradually adding sugar, and continue until mixture is thick. Add remaining ingredients and mix well. Chill 1 hour. Drop by half teaspoonfuls onto greased or foil-covered cookie sheet. Bake at 325 ° F oven about 25 minutes.

PINE NUT COOKIES

2 eggs
3/4 cup sugar
1-1/8 cup flour
1/8 t salt

1/2 t grated lemon rind
few drops of anise oil
confectioners sugar
1/4 cup pine nuts

These cookies do not contain butter. Put eggs and sugar on top of double boiler. Beal with egg beater over hot water until the mixture is lukewarm. Remove from hot water; beat until foamy and cool. Add lemon rind, anise, and fold in the flour and salt. Drop by tea-spoonfuls onto a greased and floured cookie sheet. Sprinkle with confectioners sugar and pine nuts. Let stand 10 minutes; then bake at 375° F for about 10 minutes.

CHOCOLATE DIAMONDS

3 squares of chocolate
3/4 cup butter
1-1/2 cup sugar
3 unbeaten eggs

1/2 t salt
1/2 t vanilla
3/4 cup sifted flour
3/4 cup chopped nuts

Melt chocolate and butter over hot water; add other ingredients and mix well. Spread out onto two foil-lined cookies sheets. Sprinkle with nuts and bake at 375° F for about 14 minutes. Cool slightly; then cut into 1-1/2-in diamond shapes.

MAILANDERLI

1 cup soft butter
4 eggs
1 cup sugar
grated rind of 1 lemon
4 cups sifted flour

1 cup almonds, blanched and
   grated
4 cups sifted flour
1 egg yolk mixed with 1 T cold
   water

Cream butter and sugar together and add eggs and lemon rind. Mix well and add ground almonds and flour. Chill overnight. Roll out on floured board to 1/4-in thickness. Using cookie cutters, cut into stars, bells, hearts, wreaths, and so forth, and place on greased cookie sheets. Brush with egg yolk and water. Bake at 325° F for about 15 minutes.

CHRISTMAS CUT-OUT COOKIES

1 cup butter
1 cup sugar
2 eggs, beaten

1 t vanilla
3-1/2 cups sifted flour
1 t salt

Cream together butter and sugar; add eggs and vanilla. Sift together flour and salt. Mix everything together; cover bowl, and chill for 1 hour. Roll out small amounts of dough at a time on a lightly floured board. Cut out with floured cutters. Bake on ungreased cookie sheets at 375° F for 8 minutes. Frost or decorate as wanted. Yield: 60 cookies.

PECAN DAINTIES

1 cup soft butter
1/2 cup sugar
2 cups sifted whole wheat pastry
   flour or white flour

1 t vanilla extract
1 T water
2 cups pecans, ground
Pecan halves

Cream butter and sugar until light; add remaining ingredients except pecan halves. Mix well; chill until firm. Shape into 3/4-in balls. Arrange on un-greased cookie sheets. Top each with a pecan half. Bake in 325° F oven for 20 minutes. Makes 6-8 dozen.

RUM BALLS

2 cups crushed vanilla wafers
1-1/2 cups confectioners sugar
2 cups pecans, ground fine

1/3 cup cocoa
1/4 cup corn syrup
1/2 cup rum

Combine wafer crumbs, confectioners sugar, 1 cup of ground pecans, and cocoa. Add corn syrup and rum. Roll out on foil or wax paper and cut into 1-in squares; then form these into 1-in balls; roll in remaining nuts.

AMARETTI MACAROONS

1/2 lb sugar
1/4 lb blanched almonds

1/2 t almond extract
2 egg whites

Chop and pulverize the almonds and mix thoroughly with half the sugar and the almond extract. Beat egg whites until very stiff. Add remainder of sugar; beat again. Add almond mixture and mix thoroughly. Shape into balls or cookies about 2-in in diameter. Place on greased cookie sheet about 1 in apart. Bake in 350° F oven about 5 minutes or until light brown.

SWEDISH ALMOND TARTS

Dough:
1 cup butter
1/2 cup sugar
1 egg, well beaten
2 cups flour
1 t vanilla

Filling:
2 cups almonds, ground fine
1/2 cup sugar
2 eggs, well beaten
1 t almond extract

Cream butter and sugar; mix in egg, flour, and vanilla; beat until smooth. Chill 15 minutes. Then shape into small cups, using mini-tart pans, and chill while making the filling. Blend the filling ingredients together. Then drop 1 T into each cup of dough.. Bake at 310° F oven for 25-30 minutes or until slightly brown.

NOTE: Need 6 mini-cupcake tins of 12 cupcakes each.

Flora Chiarello Menges age 59 (1972)
Born August 29, 1913 Albany, NY

Chapter VII

CAKES, PIES & OTHER SWEETS

TWELFTH NIGHT CAKE

1 cup softened unsalted butter
1 cup sugar
2 eggs, beaten
1 T grated orange peel
2-1/2 cups sifted flour
1 t baking soda
1/2 t salt
1 cup buttermilk
1/2 cup chopped glacéd fruit mix

1 cup chopped toasted walnuts
   or pecans
3/4 cup fresh squeezed orange
   juice
2 T rum
2 t fresh squeezed lemon juice
1 cup sugar
One whole blanched almond

Cream together butter and sugar; add eggs, orange and lemon peel, and beat well. Sift together flour, baking powder, soda, and salt; then add to creamed mixture alternating with the buttermilk. Beat until smooth. Stir in fruit mix, nuts, and the whole almond. Spoon batter into a well-greased 10-inch Bundt or tube pan. Bake at 350° F for 1 hour or until toothpick comes out clean. In a saucepan combine the remaining sugar, orange juice, lemon juice and rum, and bring to a boil Slowly pour this over the hot cake in the pan. Let stand 24 hours in the pan before removing and serving. Yield: 12-16 servings.

NOTE: Twelfth Night is the evening of January fifth, preceding Twelfth Day, the eve of the Epiphany, the last day of the Christmas festivities, and observed as a time of merriment. Whoever finds the almond will be married within a year.

MYRTIS'S POUND CAKE

2 cups sifted flour
1 lb confectioners' sugar
5 eggs

1/2 lb unsalted butter
1/2 t almond extract
1 t vanilla

Have all ingredients at room temperature. Mix together and beat for
5 minutes. Put in a lightly greased tube pan or in 2 loaf pnans. Bake
1 hour at 350° F. Cool in pan for at least 20 minutes.

CRUMB CRUST

9 graham crackers
1 cup toasted walnuts
4-6 T butter, cold, but chopped up into small pieces
3 T sugar
1/4 t salt

Begin by toasting the nuts in an ungreased iron skillet. Meanwhile
break the graham crackers into little pieces and blend in a Cuisinart.
Set aside. When the walnuts smell roasted & toasted, blend them in
the Cuisinart and add to the graham cracker meal. Mix carefully.
Return half of this mixture to the Cuisinart with the butter pieces
and blend; then add this to the remaining nuts and graham cracker
mixture. Oil a 9-in pie plate and turn the contents of the bowl into
the pie plate. Pat the mixture so that it forms sides and a bottom—a
pie-crust shape. Place in a preheated 350°-375° F oven for 15-20
minutes. Don't let it burn!

CHOCOLATE KAHLUA CAKE

1-3/4 cup flour
1 cup sugar
3/4 cup sweet Ghirardelli cocoa
2 t baking powder
1 t salt
1 t baking soda
2 eggs

1 cup strong black coffee
1 cup buttermilk or yoghurt
1 cup melted butter
1/3 cup buttermilk powder
1 t vanilla
1/2 cup Kahlua

Mix dry ingredients in one bowl and liquid ingredients in another. Blend the two and pour into two 10-in cake tins. Bake at 350ºF for 1 hour or until a toothpick comes out clean. Sprinkle the Kahlua over the cake and let cool.

MOCHA FILLING: Mix together in a chilled bowl 1 cup heavy cream, 1/4 cup light brown sugar, 1 T strong black coffee and 1/2 t vanilla. Beat on high until whipped.

FUDGE ICING: Place 1/2 cup sugar and 1 cup heavy cream in a heavy saucepan and stir, cooking unitl the mixture reaches the boiling point; then cook for 5 minutes. Remove from heat and add 1/2 lb semisweet chocolate, 1/2 cup butter, and 1/2 t vanilla.

Your choice—use filling, or icing, or both!

—*Mildred Spinoza*

CARROT CAKE

3 cups unbleached white flour
3 cups sugar
1 t salt
1 T baking soda
1 T ground cinnamon
1-1/2 cups vegetable oil
4 large eggs, lightly beaten

1-1/2 cups chopped toasted
    walnuts
1-1/2 cups shredded coconut
1-1/3 cups puréed carrots
1/4 cup drained crushed pine-
    apple

Preheat oven to 350°F. Grease two 9-in cake pans lined with parchment paper. Sift dry ingredients into a bowl. Add oil, eggs and vanilla, and beat well. Fold in walnuts, coconut, carrots and pineapple. Pour batter into pans and set on middle rack of the oven. Bake for 30-35 minutes or until toothpick comes out clean. Cook on a cake rack for 3 hours.

CREAM CHEESE FROSTING

8 oz cream cheese
6 T unsalted butter
3 cups confectioners' sugar

Grated rind of 1/2 lemon
Juice of 1/2 lemon

Cream together cream cheese and butter. Slowly sift in confectioners' sugar; mixture should be free of lumps. Stir in grated lemon rind and the juice of 1/2 lemon.

FLORA'S RICOTTA TART

Crust:
1 cup flour
1/4 cup sugar

1/4 cup unsalted butter
1 large egg, beaten
1 T grated orange rind

Preheat oven to 300° F. Mix all together to form a ball. Then knead gently until smooth. Wrap in plastic and chill. Roll out to fit an 9-inch pie plate and chill while preparing the filling. NOTE: The filling will make two tarts and will require two crusts.

Filling:
3 eggs well beaten
1/4 cup sugar
3/4 cup cream or milk
1 lb ricotta
1 T flour
Grated orange or lemon peel
    (optional)

Almond or vanilla extract or
    rum to taste
1/2 cup mixed fruits or light or
    dark raisins
Blanched almond halves or pine
    nuts

Mix filling ingredients in the order given until smooth and well blended. Pour into unbaked pie shell. Bake 1 hour or until firm.

For a larger tart, use 4 eggs, 1/3 c sugar, 1-1/2 lb ricotta, 1-1/4 c milk or cream, 2 T flour, and seasoning and fruit to taste. blanched almond halves, or pine nuts or rum to taste.

NOTE: If using Crumb Crust on page 91, it should be doubled for this filling. The filling will make two tarts.

SEATTLE TRAIL SNACKS

1/4 oz green powder, pulverized in a spice mill
1/2 cup unsalted melted butter
2 eggs, beaten
1/4 cup honey or rice syrup
3-4 dried apricots*
3-4 dried mango slices (soften in 1/4 cup boiling water)*

8 oz chopped dates or raisins*
1/2 cup chopped toasted walnuts
1/4 cup whole wheat pastry flour
1/4 cup buckwheat flour
1/4 cup wheat germ
1/4 cup corn meal
1/2 t baking powder
1 t 4-spice powder**

Set oven to 350° F. Oil an 8x8 pan; cut parchment paper to fit the bottom. Toast walnuts in a hot iron skillet, turning until browned. Melt butter; add green powder and stir well; add honey or brown rice syrup and beaten eggs. In a separate bowl, mix the dried ingredients—flours, baking powder, 4-spice power. When nuts are cooled, chop fine and add to dry ingredients.

Use 8 oz dates or raisins chopped fine, or substitute chopped apricots or mango slices. Vary dried fruits according to what is on hand for 1 cup total. Mix dry fruits with other dry ingredients. Combine melted butter, eggs, etc. with dry ingredients and stir.; this will be a thick mixture. Spread into pan with a rubber spatula. Bake for 15 minutes. Check with a toothpick. If it does not come out clean, increase heat to 375° F and bake 6 more minutes, using a timer. Do not overcook, but the toothpick must come out clean. When cool, cut into a tic-tac-toe pattern. Yield: 9 trail snacks. 1/2 trail snack will boost you 1750 feet of elevation gain or 2 uphill miles on the trail.

**NOTE: See instructions for 4-spice powder, page 104.

—GC, Spring 2010

MINCE MEAT PIE

1/2 lb chopped tart apples
   (Northern Spy is good)
1/2 lb currants
1/2 lb Sultana raisins
1/2 lb dark raisins
1/2 lb granulated sugar (scant)
1/4 lb candied citron
1/2 lb broken nut meats
2 oz candied orange rind

2 oz candied lemon rind
1/2 lb chopped suet
1/4 t cloves
3/4 t nutmeg
3/4 t cinnamon
Pinch mace
Pinch allspice
2 oz brandy

Mix everything together and Cook slowly for 2 hours, stirring frequently. Then seal into sterile jars. Age in a cool place for 4 weeks.

Prepare a pie crust of your liking and add the mincemeat. Bake at 450° F for 10 minutes; then at 350° F for another 30 minutes or so.

NOTE: Can pour Rum or Brandy Sauce (page 102) over this pie.

RHUBARB PIE

4 cups peeled rhubarb cut in 1/2
   -in pieces
1 cup chopped apples or 2/3 cup
   applesauce
1 cup sugar
2 T flour
1/2 T tapioca

1 beaten egg
1 T butter
1/4 cup orange juice
Grated orange and/or lemon
   rind
1 beaten egg white

Prepare pastry dough for a 2-crust 9-in pie. Roll out slightly more than half the dough and line the pie pan and coat the bottom with beaten egg white. Mix together the flour, tapioca, beaten egg, orange juice and citrus rind. Place the rhubarb and chopped apples in the unbaked shell and sprinkle with sugar; then pour beaten egg mixture over the fruit, and dot with butter. Cut remaining pie dough into 1/2-in strips for a lattice top. Bake at 475° F for 10-15 minutes; then reduce heat to 375° for 40 minutes or until the filling is bubbling.

ZUCCHINI BREAD

3 cups flour
1 t baking powder
1 t baking soda
1 t salt
3 eggs, beaten
2/3 cup vegetable oil or butter
1-1/2 cup sugar

1-1/2 t vanilla
2 cups shredded zucchini (about
   2 medium zucchini)
2 T grated fresh ginger
2 t grated lemon rind
1 cup chopped walnuts

Preheat oven to 350°F. Grease and flour 3 small or 2 large loaf pans. Combine the flour, baking powder and salt in one bowl. In a second bowl, beat the eggs, vegetable oil and sugar and vanilla for 30 seconds with an electric mixer. Stir in lemon juice, zucchini, ginger and lemon peel Gradually add this to flour mixture and pour batter into the pans. Bake 1-1/4 hour or until a toothpick comes out clean and cake pulls away from the side of the pan.

NOTE: Zucchini can be replaced with ripe mashed bananas or cooked pumpkin, although pumpkin (unless it is a sugar pumpkin) may require 2 or more cups of sugar.

ICING: Can cover with Cream Cheese Frosting (page 93).

AUNT ELLIE'S PRUNE CAKE

1/2 cup butter
1 cup sugar,
1 or 2 eggs, beaten
1 t vanilla
1 cup prune juice
1 cup mashed prunes
2 cups flour

1/2 t salt
1 t baking soda
1-1/2 t cinnamon
1/2 t allspice
1/2 t cloves
1/2-1 cup chopped walnuts

Cream butter and sugar, then add eggs and vanilla, followed by prune juice and mashed prunes. Separately mix together the flour, salt, spices, and nuts. Slowly add the sugar/prune mixture to the flour, beating carefully. Pour into a tube pan and bake at 350° F for an hour or until a toothpick comes out clean.

BREAD PUDDING

3 T soft butter
4-5 slices of bread, 1/2-in thick
3 egg yolks, slightly beaten
1/2 cup sugar
1/8 t salt
1/4 t nutmeg
1/4 cinnamon

3 cups milk
1 t vanilla
6 T sugar
3 egg whites, stiffly beaten
1/2 cup raisins

Butter the bread and arrange in baking dish. Combine egg yolks, 1/2 cup sugar, salt, spices, milk and vanilla, and stir until sugar is dissolved. Pour over bread. Sprinkle bread slices with the raisins. Place baking dish in a pan of hot water and bake at 325° F until custard begins to set, about 40 minutes. Meanwhile gradually fold 6 T osugar into stiffly beaten egg whites and continue beating to form a thick meringue. Spread over hot bread pudding and return to oven until lightly browned, about 10 minutes.

PLUM PUDDING WITH RUM or BRANDY SAUCE

1/2 cup chopped dates
3/4 cup dark raisins
1/4 cup golden raisins
1/4 cup chopped candied citron
1/4 cup chopped candied fruits
1/4 cup chopped candied orange
    rind
1-1/2 cups beer
4 eggs
1-1/2 cups firmly packed brown
    sugar

1/2 cup chopped nuts
1/2 cup fine dry bread crumbs
1/4 lb minced suet or 1 stick but-
    ter
1 cup flour
1 t salt
1-1/2 t baking powder
1 t fresh ground cinnamon
1/8 t ea: ground cloves and all-
    spice

Combine fruits and orange rind in a bowl; add beer and let stand for
1 hour. Beat eggs with brown sugar, and add fruit-beer mixture.
Stir in nuts, crumbs, and suet. Sift dry ingredients and spices; stir
into fruit mixture. Turn into 4 well-greased pint or 2 quart pudding
molds, filling them 3/4 full. Cover tightly with aluminum foil; tie se-
curely. Put on rack in deep kettle; pour boiling water to 1/2 the
depth of the molds. Cover; steam for 2-1/2 hours, adding more water as necessary. Remove from steamer; immediately remove foil
covers. Cool.

See RUM or BRANDY SAUCE recipe (page 102).

RUM or BRANDY SAUCE

6 T corn starch
1/4 t salt
1 cup sugar
2 cups water
3 eggs

2 T butter
2 t grated lemon rind
5 T lemon juice
1/4 cup rum or brandy

Combine cornstarch, salt, and 1/2 cup sugar in a double boiler. Set aside 6 t of sugar. Add water gradually, cover, and cook 10 minutes, stirring occasionally. Combine 3 unbeaten egg yolks and remaining sugar, and stir into the cornstarch/water mixture, stirring constantly. Remove from heat and add butter and, lemon rind, and cool without stirring. Beat egg whites until stiff, gradually adding 6 t sugar. Add rum or brandy and fold into the cooled mixture. Serve over plum pudding (page 101) or mincemeat pie (page 96).

CANDIED ORANGE PEEL

1/2 lb orange peel
1 cup sugar

1/2 cup water

Slice the orange peel into narrow strips and remove any white membrane. Combine sugar and water in a small saucepan. Place over high heat and bring to a boil. Then add the orange slices and turn heat to medium-high. Stir occasionally. The sugar/water combination will "candy" the orange peels after about 15-20 minutes.

PECAN BRITTLE

1-1/2 cups sugar
1 cup water
1 cup light corn syrup
1-1/2 cups chopped pecans

3 T butter
1 t vanilla
1-1/2 t baking soda

Generously butter a cookie sheet. In a large saucepan over high heat, cook sugar, water, and corn syrup until mixture reaches 280° F on a candy thermometer. Slowly add nuts and stir until temperature reaches 300° F. (The caramel gets extremely hot, so be careful when stirring and adding the nuts; don't allow this mixture to splatter.) Turn off heat. Carefully stir in the butter and vanilla until blended; then add baking soda, and stir vigorously, but cautiously. Pour mixture onto prepared cookie sheet and spread as thinly as possible with a wooden spoon. Cool for about 15 minutes. Break cooled candy into pieces and store in an airtight container. Yield: 2 lbs of pecan brittle.

USEFUL TIPS

Can Size	Volume of Food	Weight of Food
No. 1	1+1/4 cups	10+1/2 - 12 oz.
No. 300	1+3/4 cups	14 - 16 oz.
No. 303	2 cups	16 - 17 oz.
No. 2	2+1/2 cups	20 oz.
No. 2+1/2	3+1/2 cups	27 - 29 oz.
No. 3	5+3/4 cups	51 oz.
No. 10	3 quarts	6+1/2 lb. - 7 lb ; 5 oz.

WHY DO SOME FOODS "SET UP"? Foods made with onions and garlic are invariably better the next day. Why? Because although onion and garlic aromatics penetrate liquids quickly, they require additional time to penetrate solids such as pasta, rice and meat. (Explanation by Alan Granger Singer, PhD chemist)

BUYING PARMESAN CHEESE: Don't buy Parmesan cheese with a half-inch or more of white at the rind. This is a sign the cheese has dried out. The area next to the rind should be yellow. An eighth-inch or quarter-inch of white at the rind may be acceptable, if there are no better cheeses available.

TOASTING SEEDS, SPICES and/or NUTS: Toasting these ahead of time in a hot black iron skillet brings out their flavor.

GRINDING WHOLE SPICES: Grinding spice seeds, bark, etc. (after toasting them first) yields much better flavor than using pre-ground store-bought spices.

4-SPICE POWDER: This is a mixture of equal amounts of cinnamon bark, cloves, anise seeds, and nutmegs. Toast the spices; then ground fine in a spice mill. Cinnamon bark and nutmegs should be placed in a small muslin bag and smashed with a hammer before toasting and grinding. The muslin bag will keep the pieces from flying around the kitchen.

SUBSTITUTIONS YOU MAY NOT HAVE THOUGHT OF: Dried sweetened cranberries can substitute for raisins. Roasted or steamed eggplant can substitute for mushrooms.

WHITE AND WHOLE WHEAT FLOUR: Replace some wheat flour in baked goods with other flours—buckwheat, teff, millet, quinoa, potato, garbanzo bean, etc. Experiment.

ROUX: This is French for a beaten mixture of flour and water, i.e., "paste."

ABBREVIATIONS USED IN THIS BOOK:
  t = teaspoon   lb = pound
  T = tablespoon   pkg = package
  FCM = Flora Chiarello Menges   GC = Gail Chiarello

WRITE IN YOUR COOKBOOKS. Make note of your substitutions and experiments and date them. They are your books, so take control!

INDEX

Amaretti macaroons, 87
Anise biscuits, 79
Antipasti, 26
Apfelkuchen, 19
Asparagus, 48
Beans & Greens, 49
Beef
    Barbequed hamburgers, 69
    Chili, 71
    Flora's corned beef, 73
    Pa's marinated steaks, 69
    Sauerbraten, 70
    Tamale pie, 72
Beets, pickled, 28
Biscotti al'anici, 79
Black bean soup, 35

Bow-tie cookies, 81
Brandy sauce, 102
Bread pudding, 100
Bread sticks, 23
Broccoli rabe [see also Rapini] 49
Broccoli, Cream of, soup, 36
Cabbage, Sweet & sour red, 53
Cakes,
    Twelfth Night cake, 90
    Myrtis's pound cake, 91
    Chocolate Kahlua cake, 92
    Carrot cake, 93
    Aunt Ellie's prune cake, 99
Candied orange peel, 102
Caponata, Flora's, 30
Carrot cake, 93
Cauliflower, Cream of, soup, 36
Chicken cacciatore, 63
Chicken livers with sage, 64
Chicken with dumplings, 65
Chicken, Alba's champagne, 66
Chili, 71
Chocolate almond drops, 83
Chocolate diamonds, 84
Chocolate Kahlua cake, 92
Christmas cut-out cookies, 85
Cinnamon twists, 21
Cole slaw, 30
Cookies
    Amaretti macaroons, 87
    Anise biscuits, 79
    Biscotti al'anici, 79

Bow-tie cookies, 82
Chocolate almond drops, 83
Chocolate diamonds, 84
Christmas cut-out cookies, 85
Farfalle, 82
Mailanderli, 85
Pecan dainties, 84
Rum balls, 86
Swedish almond tarts, 87
Tarallini, 80
Tarallini, diagram, 81
Thimble cookies, 83
Corned beef hash, 14
Corned beef, Flora's, 73
Cottage cheese pancakes, 16
Cranberry muffins, 17
Cream cheese frosting, 93
Crumb crust, 91
Cucumber salad, 27
Dawne's navy bean soup, 37
Easter soup, 39
Eggplant parmigiana, 45
Eggplant, 44-45
Endive & radicchio salad, 29
Escarole, 47
Farfalle, 82
French onion soup, 34
Frisée, 31
Gatto di patate alla calabrese, 47
Greek zucchini & pasta, 51
Hamburgers, barbequed, 69
Kartoffelsalat, 29

Kugelhupf, 18
Lamb stew, Flora's, 75
Lasagna, 58-59
Lentil soup, 35
Mailanderli, 85
Marinara sauce, 56
Mince meat pie, 96
Minestra di Pasqua, 39
Myrtis's pound cake, 91
Navy bean soup, 37
Onion soup, French, 34
Orange peel, candied, 102
Paradise soup, 34
Pasta e fagioli, 54
Pasta with red pepper tomato
sauce, 55
Pecan brittle, 103
Pecan dainties, 86
Peppers & eggplant, 44
Peppers, veal and, Flora's, 67
Piecrust, see Crumb crust, 95
Pies
    Flora's Ricotta Pie, 94
    Mince meat pie, 96
    Rhubarb pie, 97
    Crumb crust, 91
Pine nut cookies, 84
Pizza, 54
Pizzelle, 78
Plum pudding, 101
Popovers, 20
Pork chops & sauerkraut, 74

Potato cake of Calabria, 47
Potato casserole, 52
Potato pancakes, 15
Potato rolls, 22
Potato salad, German hot, 29
Potato soup with beef stock, 38
Potatoes, roasted with onions, 50
Pound cake, Myrtis's, 91
Prosciutto, 48
Prune cake, Aunt Ellie's, 99
Pudding,
    bread, 100
    rum, 101
Radicchio, 31
Rapini, 42
Rhubarb pie, 97
Ricotta Pie, Flora's 94
Risotto Milanese, 48
Roasted red pepper sauce, 55
Roasted vegetables, 52
Rum balls, 86
Rum sauce, 102
Salad dressing, 27
Sauces
    Marinara, 55
    Roasted red pepper tomato, 57
    Lasagna, 58
    Pizza, 54
    Rum sauce, 102
    Brandy sauce, 102
Sauerbraten, 70

Sauerkraut, pork chops &, 74
Spinach, Roman-style, 43
Split pea soup, 35
Steaks, Pa's marinated, 69
Swedish almond tarts, 87
Sweet & sour red cabbage, 53
Tamale pie, 72
Tarallini, 80
Tarallini, making (diagram), 81
Thimble cookies, 83
Tomato sauce, see Marinara
sauce, 56
Trail snacks, 95
Twelfth Night cake, 90
Veal and peppers, Flora's, 67
Veal scaloppine Marsala, 68
Zucchini and pasta, Greek, 51
Zucchini bread, 98
Zucchini frittata, 46
Zuppa di Paradiso, 34

BON APPETIT!